An Elected Official's Guide to the

NEW GOVERNMENTAL FINANCIAL REPORTING MODEL

By Stephen J. Gauthier

GOVERNMENT FINANCE OFFICERS ASSOCIATION

First printing, March 2000
Second printing, June 2000
Third printing, July 2001
Fourth printing, September 2001
Fifth printing, August 2002

CONTENTS

vi Exhibits

vii Foreword

ix Preface

1 Introduction

6 **PART 1: BACKGROUND AND OVERVIEW**
What is a financial reporting model?
How many financial reporting models are there?
Why has there been a need for a separate governmental
financial reporting model?
What are the key differences between the governmental
financial reporting model and the financial reporting
model used for private-sector business enterprises?
Why was there a perceived need for a new governmental
financial reporting model?
What is the basic structure of the new governmental
financial reporting model?

23 **PART 2: KEY COMPONENTS OF THE NEW MODEL**

23 **Management's Discussion and Analysis (MD&A)**
What is the purpose of management's discussion and
analysis?
What specific types of information can be found in MD&A?
Does MD&A have the same level of reliability as the basic
financial statements?

26 **Government-wide financial statements**
What are the government-wide financial statements?
What is the purpose of the government-wide financial
statements?

What is included as part of the government-wide financial statements?

Why are governmental activities reported separate from business-type activities?

What is the meaning of a deficit balance in unrestricted net assets?

Does a positive balance in unrestricted net assets mean that a government has money to spend?

How should the net cost information presented on the government-wide statement of activities be interpreted?

What are extraordinary items and special items, and why are they reported separate from revenues and expenses?

41   Governmental Fund Statements

What are the governmental fund financial statements?

What is the purpose of the governmental fund financial statements?

What is the meaning of a deficit unreserved fund balance?

What is the meaning of an excess of expenditures over revenues in a governmental fund?

Why are the numbers that appear in the governmental fund financial statements different from those that appear for governmental activities in the government-wide financial statements?

53   Proprietary Fund Statements

What are the basic financial statements for proprietary funds?

Should all enterprise funds be self-supporting?

What is the meaning of a significant ongoing surplus or deficit in an internal service fund?

59   Fiduciary Fund Statements

What are the basic financial statements for fiduciary funds?

Does a positive balance in net assets for a defined benefit pension trust fund indicate that the plan is fully funded?

62   Required Supplementary Information

What are the essential components of a budgetary comparison?

What is the meaning of a significant difference between the original budget and the final amended budget?

How should variances be interpreted in the budgetary comparison?

What are the purpose and meaning of the required
supplementary information presented for defined benefit
pension plans?
What are the purpose and meaning of the required
supplementary information presented for infrastructure
assets?

71 **APPENDIX A**

Comparison of the Traditional and New Governmental
Financial Reporting Models

73 **APPENDIX B**

Index

EXHIBITS

4 Implementation Schedule for Provisions of GASB Statement No. 34

7 **Exhibit 1** Scope of the financial reporting model

9 **Exhibit 2** Financial reporting models encountered in practice

17 **Exhibit 3** Key improvements resulting from the new governmental financial reporting model

19 **Exhibit 4** Basic financial statements under the new governmental financial reporting model

21 **Exhibit 5** The new governmental financial reporting model

22 **Exhibit 6** Relationship of the financial reporting model to the comprehensive annual financial report

28 **Exhibit 7** Elements of the government-wide statement of net assets

29 **Exhibit 8** Basic structure of the government-wide statement of activities

43 **Exhibit 9** Structure of the governmental fund balance sheet

52 **Exhibit 10** Key differences between the governmental fund financial statements and the government-wide financial statements

56 **Exhibit 11** Common differences between operating income and cash flows from operating activities

66 **Exhibit 12** Nature of the unfunded actuarial accrued liability

FOREWORD

In June 1999, the Governmental Accounting Standards Board (GASB) established a new framework for the financial reports of state and local governments. This new framework or financial reporting model represents the biggest single change in the history of governmental accounting and financial reporting. It affects *all* state and local governments that issue financial reports in conformity with generally accepted accounting principles.

The adoption of a new governmental financial reporting model is not just a matter for accountants and auditors. Because the information in state and local government financial reports is so important, a basic understanding of the financial reporting model is essential for anyone connected with public finance, and especially for decision makers such as elected officials. This publication is designed to meet the needs of elected officials and other potential users of state and local government financial reports who may need or desire a concise, nontechnical overview of the new model. It also should be useful to accounting and auditing professionals in their efforts to explain the model to others.

It is important that elected officials and other decision makers be able to understand and fully profit from all that the new governmental financial reporting model has to offer. The Government Finance Officers Association (GFOA) hopes that this publication will contribute to achieving that objective.

GFOA wishes to thank Stephen J. Gauthier, Director of the GFOA Technical Services Center, for writing this publication. We hope this booklet, along with others in the *Elected Official's Guide* series, will provide needed guidance to elected officials seeking to improve the financial management of their governments.

Jeffrey L. Esser
Executive Director
Government Finance Officers Association
February 2000

PREFACE

GASB Statement No. 34, *Basic Financial Statements — and Management's Discussion and Analysis — for State and Local Governments*, changed forever the structure and content of state and local government financial reports. Understanding a change of this magnitude is a daunting task, especially for elected officials and others who may not have an extensive background in public-sector accounting and finance. This publication is designed to meet the specific needs of such lay users of state and local government financial reports.

The introduction to this publication provides a brief, narrative overview of the new governmental financial reporting model. It includes a table indicating when different-sized governments are required to implement the various provisions of the new model. Readers are strongly encouraged to read this introduction before proceeding to the questions and answers that follow.

The questions and answers describe in practical terms all key features of the new governmental financial reporting model. Perhaps even more important, they also address a number of analytical issues that may arise in connection with this model. For example, how should financial statement users interpret a deficit balance in unrestricted net assets in the new government-wide financial statements? Does a positive balance in that same account indicate that a government has money to spend? Why must care be taken in using the cost information provided in the government-wide statement of activities?

A number of exhibits are provided to enhance discussion of several key issues. In addition, the appendices in this guide furnish a chart identifying key differences between the old and new financial reporting models, as well as a detailed index for users desiring quick access to specific information.

For reviewing the manuscript and offering suggestions for improvement, I gratefully acknowledge Gregory S. Allison, Institute of Government, University of North Carolina at Chapel Hill; E. Barrett (Barry) Atwood Sr., Ft. Lauderdale (Florida) Airport Authority; David R. Bean, Governmental Accounting Standards Board; Douglas R. Ellsworth, Village of Mount Prospect, Illinois; Dr. Robert J. Freeman, Governmental Accounting Standards Board and Texas Technical University; Robert Scott, City of Carrollton, Texas; Robert V. Stout, City of Modesto, California; and Jon A. Wise, State of Michigan. It also is my pleasure to thank Jake W. Lorentz and James Falconer of GFOA's staff, who assisted in the same way, as well as Sheryl Feminis and the other individuals who helped throughout the editing and production process.

Stephen J. Gauthier
February 2000

Introduction

In June 1999, the Governmental Accounting Standards Board (GASB) issued Statement No. 34, *Basic Financial Statements — and Management's Discussion and Analysis — for State and Local Governments*. That pronouncement established a whole new financial reporting framework, or governmental financial reporting model, for state and local governments. The result is the biggest change in the history of public-sector accounting and financial reporting. The purpose of this publication is to help elected officials and other potential users of state and local government financial statements to understand the new governmental financial reporting model so they can fully utilize its many benefits.

Background. The traditional financial reporting model for state and local governments has roots in the early decades of the twentieth century. The National Council on Governmental Accounting (NCGA) gave this traditional model its definitive form in NCGA Statement 1, *Governmental Accounting and Financial Reporting Principles* (1979). There is little argument that NCGA Statement 1 contributed greatly to standardization and improvement of accounting and financial reporting for state and local governments. A consensus gradually emerged that additional improvements were needed if public-sector financial reporting was to fully achieve its objective of promoting fiscal and operational accountability. This consensus led the GASB to undertake a comprehensive reexamination of the traditional financial reporting model that eventually resulted in GASB Statement No. 34 and establishment of a new governmental financial reporting model.

It would be a mistake to see GASB Statement No. 34 as discarding traditional public-sector financial reporting in favor of some entirely new form of financial reporting. Rather, the GASB has elected to incorporate many of the most popular features of traditional financial reporting into the new governmental financial reporting model. Accordingly, the GASB hopes that the new governmental financial reporting model will retain and even better serve current users of state and local government financial reports and, at the same time, attract new users whose needs were not met by the previous model.

Key features of the new model. Even though the new governmental financial reporting model has deep roots in traditional public-sector accounting and financial reporting, it offers many new features. The most important of these new features are:

- *Government-wide financial reporting.* For the first time, users of state and local government financial reports have access to government-wide financial statements that provide a clear picture of the government as a single, unified entity. These new government-wide financial statements complement rather than replace traditional fund-based financial statements.

- *Additional long-term focus for governmental activities.* Traditional reporting for tax-supported (governmental) activities has focused on *near-term* inflows, outflows, and balances of *spendable* financial resources. The new financial reporting model retains this short-term focus in the governmental fund financial statements while providing a long-term perspective on these same activities in the government-wide financial statements.

- *Narrative overview and analysis.* The new governmental financial reporting model provides financial report users with a simple narrative introduction, overview, and analysis of the basic financial statements in the form of management's discussion and analysis (MD&A).

- *Information on major funds.* It is widely agreed that fund information is most useful when presented for *individual* funds rather than for aggregations of funds (e.g., all special revenue funds). Accordingly, the new governmental financial reporting model presents individual fund data for each of a government's major funds.

- *Expanded budgetary reporting.* In the past, budgetary comparisons were based solely on the final amended budget.

Under the new governmental financial reporting model, information on the original budget also is presented. In addition, the new model eliminates aggregated budget presentations (e.g., totals for all budgeted special revenue funds) in favor of comparisons for the general fund and each individual major special revenue fund.

Infrastructure reporting. As with any major change, adoption of a new governmental financial reporting model sparked some controversy. Specifically, many preparers of state and local government financial statements generally supported the new model but were not persuaded that the proposed benefits of capitalizing and depreciating a government's general infrastructure assets (e.g., roads, bridges, dams) outweigh the related costs.

Accordingly, the Government Finance Officers Association (GFOA) has formally taken the position that each government must make its own decision on whether to comply with the infrastructure reporting provisions of GASB Statement No. 34 based on its own evaluation of the relative costs and benefits of infrastructure reporting. For governments that elect to implement the infrastructure reporting provisions of GASB Statement No. 34, GFOA recommends adopting a least-cost implementation strategy consistent with the provisions of that statement. The practical application of such a strategy would reflect the following recommendations:

- Limit the retroactive reporting requirements for infrastructure to major classes of infrastructure assets.

- Define *major classes* of infrastructure as narrowly as possible.

- Limit infrastructure reporting to assets acquired during fiscal years ended after June 30, 1980.

- Use estimates whenever possible.

- Use composite approaches to calculate depreciation expense.

- Resist vendor conversion and implementation proposals that unnecessarily raise fees by going beyond the strict requirements of GASB Statement No. 34.

Timing of implementation. The mandatory deadline for implementing the provisions of GASB Statement No. 34 depends upon each government's total revenues for its first fiscal year ending after June 15, 1999. *Total revenues* for this purpose *includes* only the governmental funds and enterprise funds of the primary government, and *excludes* other financing sources and extraordinary items. On that basis, implementation dates have been established and are listed in the accompanying Implementation Schedule for Provisions of GASB Statement No. 34.

Implementation Schedule
for Provisions of GASB Statement No. 34

Total Revenues	All Provisions of GASB Statement No. 34 Except for *Retroactive* Reporting of Infrastructure Assets	Retroactive Reporting of Infrastructure Assets
$100 Million or more	Starting fiscal years ending June 30, 2002	Starting fiscal years ending June 30, 2006
$10 Million to $100 Million	Starting fiscal years ending June 30, 2003	Starting fiscal years ending June 30, 2007
Less than $10 Million	Starting fiscal years ending June 30, 2004	Retroactive reporting of infrastructure assets *not* required

Using this guide. This guide, like others in GFOA's *Elected Official's Guide* series, is presented using a simple question-and-answer format. The questions may be approached consecutively to provide a comprehensive overview of the new governmental financial reporting model; or, users may choose to look specifically for questions and answers that most interest them. Collectively, the questions in this guide *describe* the new governmental financial reporting model as well as provide practical information on *how to evaluate and interpret the information* in the new model.

Government finance officers may wish to provide copies of this guide to their elected officials. If finance officers choose to use the material in the guide as a basis for presentations to these officials, it may still be useful to provide the officials with a copy of the guide to serve as a reference as questions arise.

Two appendices are included in this guide. Appendix A is a chart providing a brief overview of the key differences between the new reporting model and its predecessor. Appendix B is an index designed to help users easily find information on specific topics.

PART 1
BACKGROUND AND OVERVIEW

What is a financial reporting model?

Public-sector financial reports are designed to serve the needs of a wide range of users, including investors and creditors, legislative and oversight bodies, citizens, taxpayers, and the media. It is impractical for a single published financial report to provide *all* information needed or desired by such a broad range of users.

Consequently, those who prepare financial reports aim instead at providing the *basic information needed for fair presentation* of a government's finances. The criteria that accountants use to determine whether a financial report is fairly presented are known as generally accepted accounting principles (GAAP). The Governmental Accounting Standards Board (GASB) is responsible for setting GAAP for state and local governments. The Financial Accounting Standards Board establishes the criteria for private-sector business enterprises and not-for-profit organizations.

There are three ways to present required information within a financial report:

- Much of the needed data is *displayed* in the form of *financial statements*.

- These financial statements are accompanied by *disclosures* in the form of *notes to the financial statements* to ensure that a complete picture is presented in the financial statements. The financial statements and notes together form a single, integrated whole known simply as the *basic financial statements*.

- Finally, financial analysis sometimes requires certain additional information that cannot in its own right be considered essential to the fair presentation of a government's finances. Financial reports provide this extra data in the form of *required supplementary information* (RSI).

The financial statements and accompanying notes (i.e., basic financial statements) are the focus of the independent audit. RSI, on the other hand, falls outside the scope of the independent audit. The auditor, though, is required to perform certain limited procedures in connection with RSI, such as making inquiries of management regarding RSI measurement and presentation.

The term *financial reporting model* is used to describe the *minimum* set of: 1) financial statements (number, type, format, and contents); 2) note disclosures; and 3) RSI that must be presented in a financial report for an independent auditor to be able to assert, without qualification or further comment, that a government's finances are fairly presented in conformity with GAAP.

Exhibit 1 illustrates the scope of the financial reporting model.

EXHIBIT 1
Scope of the Financial Reporting Model

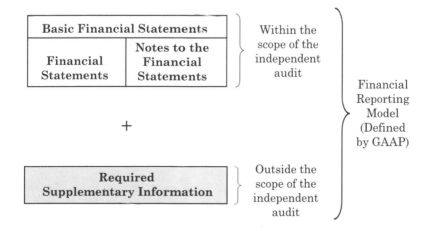

How many financial reporting models are there?

In the not-too-distant past, there existed many financial reporting models. Recently, the number of models has been reduced to three: 1) business enterprises, 2) not-for-profit organizations, and 3) state and local governments.

In the private sector, there are two separate financial reporting models: one for business enterprises and one for not-for-profit organizations. While both models prescribe three basic financial statements (a balance sheet, an operating statement, and a statement of cash flows), there are crucial differences between the two models.

The business enterprise model is designed to demonstrate the degree to which a business's capital (i.e., the investment by owners/stockholders) has been maintained. Thus, the balance sheet of a business distinguishes net assets based on whether they are the product of investment (i.e., owner's equity, capital stock, paid-in-capital in excess of par) or of earnings (i.e., retained earnings). Likewise, the operating statement of a business focuses on transactions and events that affect earnings (i.e., revenues, expenses, gains and losses).

Because not-for-profit organizations are concerned with providing services rather than making a profit, there is no presumption of an intent to preserve capital. Accordingly, the net assets of a not-for-profit organization are classified based on their availability for use in operations (e.g., investment in capital assets, restricted, unrestricted) rather than their origin (i.e., investment versus earnings). Likewise, the operating statement of a not-for-profit organization includes all transactions and events that affect the organization's net assets.

In the public sector, a single financial reporting model applies to all governmental entities. While the governmental financial reporting model is unique, it bears many similarities to the not-for-profit and business enterprise models, especially for a government's business-type or proprietary activities.

Exhibit 2 lists the three financial reporting models.

EXHIBIT 2
Financial Reporting Models Encountered in Practice

Financial Reporting Models		
Private Sector		Public Sector
Business Enterprise Model	Not-for-Profit Model	Governmental Financial Reporting Model

Why has there been a need for a separate governmental financial reporting model?

For at least two important reasons, governments have always used a financial reporting model separate from the one used by private-sector businesses and not-for-profit organizations.

First, there are important legal restrictions on how a government uses its resources. These restrictions are imposed externally (e.g., grant contracts and bond indentures) and internally (i.e., the annual or biennial operating budget). Moreover, in a government based on the separation of executive and legislative powers, even the internal restrictions imposed by the operating budget are significant. That is, the operating budget in the public sector is not just a financial plan; it also serves as a control device with legal sanctions to ensure compliance. Because governments must be accountable for their stewardship of public resources, a stated goal of governmental accounting and financial reporting has been to demonstrate compliance with finance-related legal and contractual provisions.

The second reason for a separate governmental financial reporting model is that private-sector financial reporting has always emphasized the *ultimate effect* of transactions and events of the period rather than their near-term financing implications. In the public sector, however, virtually all financial decisions are made in the context of the annual or biennial appropriated operating budget, which focuses primarily on balances and transactions associated with a government's *near-term financing*. Consequently, state and local government financial statements have placed a premium on providing information that makes sense to decision makers in the context of the operating budget's short-term financing focus.

What are the key differences between the governmental financial reporting model and the financial reporting model used for private-sector business enterprises?

Traditionally, there have been three key differences between the reporting model used by governments and the model used by private-sector businesses. These differences reflect the special public-sector emphasis on demonstrating compliance with finance-related legal and contractual provisions, as well as the desire to provide information relevant for decision making in a budgetary environment.

The key elements that distinguish the governmental financial reporting model are:

- *Fund accounting.* Governments establish separate funds to segregate financial resources that are subject to special regulations, restrictions, or limitations. These funds are presented in a government's financial report to demonstrate legal compliance.

- *Special accounting for tax-supported activities.* Traditionally, the funds used to report tax-supported or governmental activities have focused exclusively on near-term inflows and outflows of spendable financial resources, consistent with the near-term financing focus of the annual or biennial appropriated operating budget.

- *Presentation of budgetary comparison statements.* Although businesses adopt budgets as financial plans, they do not present budget-to-actual comparisons in connection with their financial reports. The budget is much more than a financial plan, however, in the public sector; there it serves also as a key control device that is backed by legal sanctions. Accordingly, given the premium that public-sector accounting and financial reporting have placed on demonstrating compliance with finance-related legal and contractual provisions, budgetary comparisons traditionally have been presented in connection with the financial reports of state and local governments.

Why was there a perceived need for a new governmental financial reporting model?

Accountability is the paramount objective of financial reporting for state and local governments. There are two separate and equally important aspects of accountability. *Fiscal accountability* requires that governments demonstrate compliance with public decisions concerning the raising and spending of public monies in the short term (usually one budgetary cycle or one year). *Operational accountability* requires that a government demonstrate the extent to which it has met its operating objectives efficiently and effectively, using all resources available for that purpose, and whether it can continue to do so.

The traditional governmental financial reporting model, with its strong emphasis on legal compliance, was generally successful at providing a high level of fiscal accountability. Over the years, however, a consensus emerged that change was needed to enhance the operational accountability component of financial reporting for state and local governments. This change came in June 1999, in the form of GASB Statement No. 34, *Basic Financial Statements — and Management's Discussion and Analysis — for State and Local Governments.*

The new financial reporting model instituted by GASB Statement No. 34 seeks to improve operational accountability by highlighting the big picture that was sometimes lost in the detail of fund accounting. Some key specific changes in this regard are:

- *Introduction of government-wide financial statements.* In the past, a government was not presented as a single, uni-

fied entity. Instead, financial reporting focused on aggregations of similar individual funds known as *fund types* (e.g.,
special revenue funds, capital projects funds). Under the
new governmental financial reporting model instituted by
GASB Statement No. 34, governments continue to provide
fund-based information. With the new model, however,
these fund-based presentations are complemented by a set
of government-wide financial statements that for the first
time present the government as a single, unified entity
comparable in many ways to a consolidated, private-sector
business enterprise.

- *Expanded focus for governmental activities.* In the past, financial reporting for tax-supported (governmental) activities focused solely on near-term inflows and outflows of
  spendable resources (consistent with the near-term financing focus of the annual or biennial appropriated operating
  budget). This same focus continues for fund-based presentations of governmental activities. Operational accountability, however, requires that financial reporting also
  address the long-term implications of near-term financing
  decisions. To do so, governmental activities are now ac-
  counted for in the same way as business-type activities in
  the new government-wide financial statements.

- *Presentation of cost data.* Operational accountability requires that a government demonstrate the extent to which
  it has met its operating objectives efficiently and effectively, using all resources available for that purpose, and
  whether it can continue to do so. An essential step toward
  this goal is calculating the *cost* of each of a government's
  functional activities (e.g., general government, public
  safety, public works). Accordingly, the new government-
  wide statement of activities provides cost information for
  both governmental and business-type activities. Pre-
  viously, no *cost* information was available in financial reports for governmental activities because of their special
  focus on near-term inflows and outflows of spendable resources. The government-wide statement of activities also
  demonstrates the degree to which each government function is self-financing (i.e., financed in whole or in part

through resources provided by customers, grantors, or contributors).

- *Narrative overview and analysis.* It is often difficult for those who are not accountants to know what to look for in a set of financial statements. This problem is especially acute in the public sector because of fund accounting. To ensure that readers do not get lost in the detail, the new financial reporting model requires that financial statements be introduced by a brief narrative overview and analysis, known as *management's discussion and analysis*, providing management's perspective on the financial picture presented in the accompanying financial statements.

The new governmental financial reporting model also seeks to improve fiscal accountability in several important ways:

- *Shift in focus to major individual funds.* As noted, past financial reporting focused on aggregations of individual funds known as *fund types*. Since each individual fund represents the segregation of resources for a specific purpose, such aggregated presentations have not been useful in demonstrating legal compliance (a primary objective of fund accounting) or for other decision-making purposes. To remedy this deficiency, the new governmental financial reporting model refocuses the fund-based presentations in the basic financial statements on *individual governmental and enterprise funds*. Since it typically is not practical to present information on each individual governmental and enterprise fund as part of the basic financial statements, the requirement to present individual fund data is limited to a government's *major* individual governmental and enterprise funds.

- *Shift in focus to individual fund budgets.* In the past, information was aggregated by fund type also for budget-to-actual comparisons associated with the basic financial statements. Once again, such aggregated information rarely proved useful for demonstrating legal compliance, a primary objective of budgetary comparison reporting. Consequently, the new governmental financial reporting model limits budgetary comparison in connection with the basic financial statements to the general fund and *major individual special revenue funds*.

- *Inclusion of data from the original budget.* The annual or biennial operating budget is not a static document. Indeed, the original appropriated budget typically is amended at least once during the fiscal year. Traditionally, budget-to-actual comparisons have focused exclusively on comparing actual results (presented on a budgetary basis) with the final amended budget. Limiting budget-to-actual comparisons to the final amended budget, however, usually confuses those familiar with the budget as originally adopted. Therefore, the new governmental financial reporting model requires that actual results be compared with both the original and the final amended budget.

Exhibit 3 summarizes the key improvements resulting from the new governmental financial reporting model.

EXHIBIT 3
Key Improvements Resulting from
the New Governmental Financial Reporting Model

Improvements Designed to Enhance Operational Accountability		Improvements Designed to Enhance Fiscal Accountability	
Previous Model	New Model	Previous Model	New Model
All reporting based on funds and fund types	Introduction of government-wide financial statements	Information in basic financial statements aggregated by fund type	Information in basic financial statements presented separately for major individual governmental and enterprise funds
Information on governmental activities limited to near-term inflows and outflows of spendable resources	Government-wide financial statements provide additional long-term focus for governmental activities	Budgetary comparisons associated with the basic financial statements aggregated by fund type	Budgetary comparisons associated with the basic financial statements presented for the general fund and individual major special revenue funds
Cost data available only for business-type activities	Cost data provided for both governmental and business-type activities	Budgetary comparisons report only final amended budget	Budgetary comparisons report both original and final amended budget
No narrative required	Narrative overview and analysis required in the form of Management's Discussion and Analysis		

What is the basic structure of the new governmental financial reporting model?

The governmental financial reporting model defines the *minimum* combination of financial statements, note disclosures, and RSI necessary for fair presentation in conformity with GAAP. The new model provides for both government-wide and fund financial statements. The fund financial statements are further subdivided into three separate categories: governmental, proprietary, and fiduciary funds. Governmental funds are used primarily to account for a government's tax-supported (governmental) activities. Proprietary funds typically are used in connection with a government's business-type (fee-supported) activities. Fiduciary funds are used to account for government-held resources that are *not* available to support the government's own programs, such as pension plan assets. A single set of note disclosures is to accompany both the government-wide and fund-based financial statements.

Exhibit 4 illustrates the basic set of financial statements under the new governmental financial reporting model, including information on each required individual financial statement.

EXHIBIT 4
Basic Financial Statements
Under the New Governmental Financial Reporting Model

Government-wide Financial Statements	Fund Financial Statements		
	Governmental Funds	Proprietary Funds	Fiduciary Funds
Statement of net assets	Balance sheet	Statement of net assets	Statement of net assets
Statement of activities	Statement of revenues, expenditures, and changes in fund balances	Statement of revenues, expenses, and changes in net assets	
	Budgetary comparison statement (optional)	Statement of cash flows	Statement of changes in net assets
NOTES TO THE FINANCIAL STATEMENTS			

The new governmental financial reporting model calls for the basic financial statements to be accompanied by several types of RSI. In all cases, the basic financial statements are to be preceded by a narrative overview and analysis in the form of management's discussion and analysis (MD&A). Additional RSI follows the notes to the financial statements in these circumstances:

- *Budgetary comparisons.* For governments that report one or more governmental funds, a budget-to-actual comparison is to be presented as RSI for the general fund and any individual major special revenue funds with appropriated annual or biennial operating budgets. Alternatively, these budgetary comparisons may be presented as part of the basic financial statements for the governmental funds. In this case, the budgetary comparisons fall within the scope of the independent audit.

- *Infrastructure data.* The new governmental financial reporting model requires that governments report their infrastructure assets on the face of the financial statements.

Infrastructure assets include roads, bridges, tunnels, drainage systems, water and sewer systems, dams, and lighting systems. Normally, capital assets including infrastructure must be depreciated. Governments, however, may avoid the requirement to depreciate a given network or subsystem of infrastructure assets by promising to maintain the network or subsystem at a condition level predetermined by the government. Governments that elect this modified approach must disclose as RSI certain information regarding the condition level of such assets, as well as a comparison of estimated and actual expenses for preservation and maintenance.

- *Pension trend data.* Governments that report pension trust funds generally are required to report certain actuarial trend data as RSI after the notes to the financial statements. A similar requirement applies to employers who participate in single-employer or agent multiple-employer pension plans. In an *agent* multiple-employer pension plan, each participating employer has a separate actuarial valuation. In contrast, in a *cost-sharing* multiple-employer pension plan, a single actuarial valuation is used to set rates for all participating employers.

- *Claims development trend data.* Public-entity risk pools are required to present as RSI certain revenue and claims development trend data.

Exhibit 5 illustrates how the basic financial statements and RSI combine to form the new governmental financial reporting model.

EXHIBIT 5
The New Governmental Financial Reporting Model

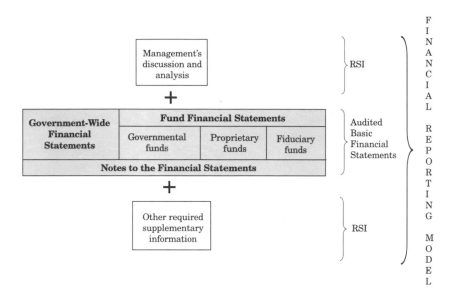

The financial reporting model is concerned with the *mini-mum* requirements for fair presentation in conformity with GAAP. Governments are encouraged, however, to go beyond these minimum requirements and to present a *comprehensive* annual financial report (CAFR).

A CAFR has three basic sections: introductory, financial, and statistical. The introductory section furnishes general information on government structure, services, and operating environment. The financial section contains all basic financial statements and RSI, as well as information on all individual funds *not* reported separately in the basic financial statements. Governments also sometimes use the financial section to provide other supplementary information that is not required. The statistical section provides trend data and nonfinancial data useful in interpreting the basic financial statements.

The CAFR and its relationship to the financial reporting model are illustrated in Exhibit 6.

EXHIBIT 6
Relationship of the Financial Reporting Model
to the Comprehensive Annual Financial Report

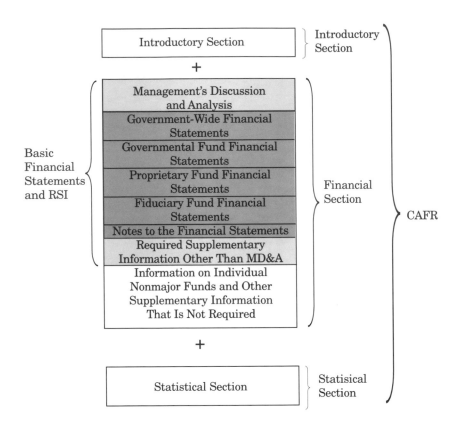

PART 2
KEY COMPONENTS OF THE NEW MODEL

Management's Discussion and Analysis

What is the purpose of management's discussion and analysis?

The role of management's discussion and analysis (MD&A) is to provide the *narrative introduction and overview* that users need to interpret the basic financial statements. MD&A also provide *analyses* of key data presented in the basic financial statements. For example, what is the explanation for significant increases or decreases in revenues or expenses? Why is the final amended budget for the general fund different from the original budget? Why have fund balances increased or decreased in the general fund?

What specific types of information can be found in MD&A?

At minimum, MD&A must provide the following information:

- Brief explanation of the types of presentations that make up the basic financial statements and their relationship to each other;

- Condensed financial information allowing readers to compare the current and prior fiscal periods. (GAAP do not require the presentation of comparative financial statements; therefore, *in many cases, this will be the sole source of government-wide comparative data in the financial report*);

- Analysis of the government's overall financial position (net assets) and results of operations (changes in net assets);

- Analysis of the balances and transactions of major individual funds;

- Analysis of variations from the original and final amended budget for the general fund;

- Significant capital asset and long-term debt activity (e.g., major capital construction and debt issues);

- Any facts, decisions, or conditions *known as of the close of audit field work* that are *expected to have a significant effect* on financial position or results of operation.

Does MD&A have the same level of reliability as the basic financial statements?

While financial statement users have good cause to rely on MD&A information, there are three reasons MD&A is not as reliable as the basic financial statements themselves.

First, to serve their intended purpose, MD&A must present *select* information. A comprehensive presentation such as the basic financial statements usually is more reliable.

Second, a key component of MD&A is the presentation of management's *analysis* of the financial information. Because a degree of subjectivity is inherent in any analytical presentation, analytical data are not as reliable as the more objective information presented in the basic financial statements.

Finally, MD&A are not included within the scope of the independent audit of the financial statements. As a result, the auditor does *not* offer an opinion regarding MD&A reliability. The independent auditor is responsible, however, for performing certain limited procedures in connection with MD&A, such as making inquiries of management regarding RSI measurement and presentation. If in conducting these procedures the auditor finds the MD&A presentation somehow deficient, the auditor must disclose the deficiency in the independent auditor's report on the fair presentation of the financial statements.

Government-wide Financial Statements

What are the government-wide financial statements?

There are two government-wide basic financial statements: the statement of net assets and the statement of activities.

The statement of net assets is used to report all that a government owns (assets) and owes (liabilities). A government's assets include financial resources such as cash, receivables, and investments. Also included are capital assets (such as land, buildings and improvements, and equipment), *including infrastructure* (such as roads, bridges, tunnels, drainage systems, water and sewer systems, dams, and lighting systems). A government's liabilities include vendor payables and various debt instruments (such as bonds, notes, and leases), as well as obligations incurred in connection with government operation (such as salaries payable, vacation leave, and claims and judgments).

There are two ways assets and liabilities can be presented in the statement of net assets. One method is to present accounts in the *order of their relative liquidity*. Using this approach, classes of assets that are more readily spendable (e.g., cash, receivables, investments) precede classes of assets less easily converted to cash (e.g., capital assets). Likewise, classes of liabilities expected to be liquidated in the near future (e.g., vendor payables) precede items expected to be liquidated at some later date (e.g., bonds payable).

The relative order of liquidity for asset and liability classes is determined by *the average of all items within a given class*. That is, there may be significant variations in liquidity for individual items within an asset or liability class. Still, any class of liabilities with an average maturity greater than one year must be reported in two components—the amount due within one year, and the amount due in more than one year.

Alternatively, governments may follow the private-sector practice of classifying assets and liabilities based on whether an individual item (rather than a class) is *current* or *long-term*. For this purpose, a current asset or liability generally is expected to mature within one year of the fiscal period end.

The difference between assets and liabilities is reported as *net assets*, a classification subdivided into three categories to indicate limitations on the use of net assets. First, a sizable portion of any government's net assets reflects the government's investment in capital assets. Therefore, a portion of net assets must be classified as *invested in capital assets, net of related debt* to indicate that this amount is not really accessible for other purposes. A second portion of net assets reflects resources not accessible for general use because their use is subject to restrictions enforceable by third parties (e.g., grant resources). Any remaining net assets are classified as *unrestricted*.

Exhibit 7 illustrates the elements of the government-wide statement of net assets.

EXHIBIT 7
Elements of the Government-Wide
Statement of Net Assets

Capital Assets	Capital-Related Debt
	Net Assets Invested In Capital Assets, Net of Related Debt
Restricted Resources	Liabilities Related to Restricted Resources
	Restricted Net Assets
Other Assets	Other Liabilities
	Unrestricted Net Assets

LEGEND:
▨ Assets
▢ Liabilities
▢ Net Assets

The **statement of activities** is used to report all changes in a government's net assets. This statement focuses on *expenses* (cost) rather than *expenditures* (near-term outflows of spendable resources). Expenses include depreciation on a government's capital assets. At a minimum, expenses are presented separately for each of the government's functional activities (e.g., general government, public safety, public works).

For a private-sector business enterprise, *revenues* is the first item in the operating statement, reflecting the universal business goal of maximizing revenues. Government operates quite differently. In the public sector, the goal is to provide needed services, not to maximize revenues. Revenues in the public sector are viewed as a means to an end (providing services) rather than as an end in themselves (profit). Consequently, the first item in the statement of activities for state and local governments is *expenses*, not *revenues*.

The full cost of government services need not be financed exclusively from a government's own resources. The cost of providing specific services may be offset by outside resources such as fees, charges, grants, and contributions. The statement of activities is presented using a net cost format designed to highlight the portion of each functional activity that must be financed from the government's own resources. The statement first reports all direct costs associated with each functional activity, then reports dedicated outside resources (program revenues) as a direct reduction to arrive at the program's net cost to the government.

Exhibit 8 illustrates the basic structure of the government-wide statement of activities.

EXHIBIT 8
Basic Structure of the Government-Wide
Statement of Activities

Total Direct Expenses by Functional Activity [A]	Less: Program Revenues			Net Expenses by Functional Activity (Net Program Cost) $A - (X+Y+Z) = [A1]$
	Fees and Charges [X]	Operating Grants and Contributions [Y]	Capital Grants and Contributions [Z]	
				General Revenues [B]
				"Special" and Similar Items [C] / "Special" and Similar Items [D]
				Increase or (Decrease) in Net Assets $B + C - (A1 + D) = [E]$

LEGEND:
⬜ Inflows
⬜ Outflows

What is the purpose of the government-wide financial statements?

There are three primary reasons why government-wide financial statements are needed along with the more traditional fund-based presentations. First, a government is more than simply the sum of its parts (funds). The presentation of a government-wide set of financial statements is a practical way of focusing users' attention on this crucial fact.

Second, governmental funds, as discussed earlier, focus solely on near-term inflows and outflows of spendable resources. While such information is vital, especially in a budgetary environment, information is still needed regarding the *total impact* of transactions and events on a government's finances. Government-wide financial reporting gives financial statement users the information they need to understand the long-term effect of the short-term financing decisions made in connection with activities reported in governmental funds.

Finally, while governments are not driven by the profit motive, they still wish to know the cost of providing different types of services. Governmental funds focus on inflows and outflows of spendable resources (expenditures) rather than cost (expenses). Therefore, financial statement users must turn to the government-wide statement of activities for cost information on activities reported in governmental funds.

What is included as part of the government-wide financial statements?

Accounting and financial reporting place a premium on economic substance over legal form. Accordingly, financial reports for state and local governments include the government as legally defined (i.e., the primary government), and any legally separate entities for which the primary government is financially accountable (i.e., component units). This combination of the primary government and component units is referred to as the *financial reporting entity*.

Not all resources of the financial reporting entity are necessarily available to support government programs of the reporting entity. Specifically, some resources may be held in a purely fiduciary capacity on behalf of third parties. No particular problem arises when such resources are included in fund-based presentations, because their fiduciary character is clearly conveyed to financial statement users by the use of one or more separate funds. Inclusion of these same resources in government-wide financial statements, however, could easily be misinterpreted as indicating that those resources are somehow available to support government programs. Therefore, to avoid any potential misunderstanding regarding the availability of fiduciary resources to support government programs, both *fiduciary funds* of the primary government and *component units of a fiduciary character* are *excluded* from the government-wide financial statements.

Why are governmental activities reported separate from business-type activities?

The net-cost format of the government-wide statement of activities is designed to highlight the extent to which each of a government's various functional activities is self-financing. Governments, however, ordinarily have different financing expectations for different activities. Most typical government activities—public safety, for example—are funded entirely or almost entirely from tax revenues. Other activities—an electric utility, for example—are financed entirely or almost entirely from user fees and charges. Still other activities, such as mass transit, are funded through a combination of fees, charges, and operating subsidies.

Presenting cost information for all of a government's functional activities together could invite unwarranted comparisons. For example, a police department is not expected to be self-financing; but a public utility that is not self-financing could signal serious financial difficulties. To assist financial statement users in making appropriate comparisons, governmental activities are reported separate from business-type activities in the government-wide financial statements. Program revenues are not expected to cover the costs of governmental activities; they *are* expected to cover at least a substantial portion of the costs of business-type activities.

What is the meaning of a deficit balance in unrestricted net assets?

Governments recognize a liability on the government-wide statement of net assets as soon as an obligation is incurred. For example, a liability for vacation leave is recognized as soon as employees earn the leave, even though a portion of the leave will not be taken (and paid for) until some subsequent period. Likewise, claims and judgments are recognized as liabilities as soon as the cause occurs, even though payment may not be made for some time.

While *accounting* is primarily concerned with when a liability is incurred, *financing* focuses on when a liability will be paid. As a rule, governments raise resources to meet their *financing needs*. That is, the resources needed to liquidate a liability typically are raised and budgeted during the year in which the liability is to be liquidated rather than during the year in which the liability is incurred.

Vacation leave best illustrates this rule. Employees routinely build up banks of unused vacation leave because they frequently earn vacation leave in one fiscal period, but take it in another. No payment occurs until the period in which the leave is actually taken. Moreover, even when employees eventually use deferred vacation leave, the leave taken is likely replaced immediately by additional amounts of deferred vacation leave. Consequently, a typical government never really pays off its liability for vacation leave. Instead, the liability normally remains and grows indefinitely. Accordingly, most governments do *not* budget vacation leave as such. Instead, they simply budget their regular payroll for each period (which includes vacation leave, since employees commonly are paid the same whether they are working or on vacation), plus any additional amounts they anticipate for termination payments for unused vacation leave.

Because governments tend to raise resources based on when liabilities are expected to be paid rather than on when they are incurred, most governments normally do *not* have sufficient *current* resources on hand to cover current *and* long-term liabilities. A deficit balance in *unrestricted net assets* reflects this situation.

The situation just described does *not* occur in the business sector, because equity related to capital assets is not reported separately, per se, from other equity. Thus, a business's equity in its capital assets is available to offset long-term accrued liabilities like compensated absences, thereby avoiding a deficit.

In summary, a deficit in unrestricted net assets should *not* be considered, *of itself*, evidence of economic or financial difficulties. Rather, the deficit simply reflects the extent to which a government has elected to defer to future periods the financing of certain liabilities, which is a matter of public policy. Of course, financial statement users value the number reported as a deficit, since it provides an excellent measure of how far the current and previous governing bodies have *already committed* the government's *future taxing power* for purposes other than capital acquisition.

Does a positive balance in unrestricted net assets mean that a government has money to spend?

Recall that *net assets invested in capital assets* are reported *net of related debt*. Of course, the capital assets against which this related debt is netted cannot actually be used to repay the debt. Rather, the amounts needed for debt service on capital-related debt must come from a combination of restricted and unrestricted net assets. Therefore, a positive balance in unrestricted net assets in no way indicates that a government has surplus resources.

This positive balance question raises the crucial issue of the relationship between the government-wide financial statements and the governmental fund financial statements. The latter, which focus on a government's near-term financing needs, must be consulted in all matters involving the availability of spendable resources.

How should the net cost information presented on the government-wide statement of activities be interpreted?

A key goal of the government-wide statement of activities is to provide financial statement users with information on the cost of each of a government's functional activities. Care must be taken, however, to properly interpret the cost information provided in the statement of activities.

Direct costs versus indirect costs. The costs reported for each of a government's functional activities generally include only those costs that can be directly associated with that particular function. Functional activities, however, often benefit substantially from indirect (overhead) costs that are reported separately as part of another functional category (e.g., general government). As a result, the amounts reported as expense for a given functional activity ordinarily do *not* represent the full cost (direct and indirect costs) of that activity.

In some cases, governments voluntarily provide the additional data needed to determine the full cost of each functional activity. Specifically, such governments present a separate column on the statement of activities—immediately following the column reporting direct costs—that allocates the government's various indirect costs to each of the benefiting functional activities. Management enjoys considerable discretion in how indirect costs are allocated in such situations. GAAP require only that indirect costs be allocated in a systematic and rational manner (e.g., relative percentage of budgeted payroll), and that the method used for allocation be disclosed in the notes to the financial statements.

Avoidable versus unavoidable costs. It is tempting to think that all costs related to a given activity could be avoided simply by eliminating that activity. As a practical matter, however, many costs related to a functional activity are *not* eliminated simply by eliminating that activity. For example, dropping a given activity typically will not produce any significant savings in payroll processing costs. Also, it is unlikely that the government office space devoted to the activity will be rented out to a third party when the activity ends. Accountants often refer to such unavoidable costs as *fixed* or *sunken* costs.

At the same time, from a long-term perspective, all costs are ultimately avoidable. For example, while it is unlikely that payroll staff will be laid off as the result of eliminating a single activity, the additional time made available by eliminating that activity might make it unnecessary to hire additional payroll staff. Similarly, office space availability resulting from termination of an activity might eliminate or delay the need for new construction.

In making cost-based decisions, it is essential to distinguish avoidable costs from unavoidable costs. Only avoidable costs can be saved, at least in the near term, by eliminating or reducing a given functional activity. This consideration is particularly important when comparing costs for purposes of making a decision whether to contract out for services currently performed by the government.

Capital costs. An important part of the cost of providing a service is the cost of the capital assets used for that purpose. Accountants calculate the cost of capital assets used in providing services by depreciating those assets over their useful service life. Depreciation is the allocation of the *historical cost* of a capital asset to each period that benefits from its use.

Because assets are reported in the financial statements at their historical cost, and because depreciation is based on historical cost, there is no natural relationship between the net book value of a capital asset (historical cost less accumulated depreciation) and its current fair value or replacement value. Nor is there any relationship between the net book value of a capital asset and its service value.

For example, because of inflation, two virtually identical buildings built 10 years apart are likely to have significantly different historical costs even though they may offer essentially the same service value (e.g., square footage of office space). This disparity is most pronounced, of course, for assets with particularly lengthy useful lives, such as buildings and infrastructure. Moreover, some governments depreciate their infrastructure assets, such as roads and bridges, while other governments are not required to do so because they use the modified approach for one or more networks or subsystems of infrastructure assets.

For these reasons, care must be taken when making cost comparisons for functional activities between governments, particularly for those activities involving substantial amounts of depreciation expense. Otherwise, financial statement users might wrongly conclude that governments with newer, more costly assets are somehow automatically less efficient than governments with older, less expensive assets. (This cost difference may be at least partially balanced, of course, by the increased costs often associated with maintaining and operating older assets.)

Depreciation expense versus replacement cost. Governments sometimes speak of *funding depreciation* on their capital assets. This means that governments sometimes set aside resources during the life of a capital asset to finance its replacement at the end of its useful life. Because depreciation is based on the historical cost of an asset, setting aside amounts equal to depreciation expense over the life of a capital asset rarely produces sufficient resources to fund its replacement. Accordingly, governments should remember that planning for the ongoing replacement of capital assets should be based on the estimated replacement cost of those assets, not upon depreciation expense.[1]

---

[1]Grantors normally are unwilling to fund the cost of replacement assets from which they may or may not benefit. Accordingly, grantors will only reimburse depreciation expense on capital assets used for grant purposes.

Depreciation expense and rate setting. While depreciation is the allocation of the historical cost of a capital asset throughout its useful life, governments often finance the acquisition of capital assets by means of debt with maturity dates considerably sooner than the end of an asset's useful life. In such cases, rates based on depreciation expense could result in significant cash flow difficulties (for instance, collecting resources over 40 years of useful life for debt payments due over 15 years). Accordingly, governments commonly use debt service requirements rather than depreciation expense for rate-setting purposes.

What are extraordinary items and special items, and why are they reported separate from revenues and expenses?

It is hard to make decisions based on financial data for a single year, so financial statement users routinely rely on trends over time in analyzing a government's financial performance. Unfortunately, certain one-time events and transactions could easily obscure such trends. Accordingly, GAAP require that such items be reported separate from a government's regular ongoing revenues and expenses.

Two types of one-time items qualify for separate reporting. An *extraordinary item* is an event unusual in nature *and* infrequent in occurrence (e.g., hurricane damage in New England). A *special item* is a transaction *subject to management's control* that is *either*—not both—unusual in nature *or* infrequent in occurrence (e.g., a major sale of park land). Extraordinary items are common to public- and private-sector financial reporting; special items are unique to government.

Either extraordinary items or special items are reported as a separate line item near the bottom of the statement of activities. If a government has extraordinary items *and* special items to report in the same year, the two types of items are reported separately.

Governmental Fund Statements

What are the governmental fund financial statements?

At least two basic financial statements are reported for governmental funds: the balance sheet, and the statement of revenues, expenditures, and changes in fund balances. Optionally, a budgetary comparison may be presented as a third basic financial statement.

Governmental fund balance sheet. Because governmental funds focus on a government's near-term financing needs, the balance sheet for governmental funds reports only the *financial* assets associated with governmental activities. Financial assets include cash as well as other assets that will convert to cash in the course of their ordinary lives (e.g., receivables and investments). Financial assets also sometimes include inventories (e.g., materials and supplies) and prepaid items (e.g., prepaid rent and insurance), which are considered financial assets not because they will convert to cash, but because they avoid near-term outflows of financial resources that otherwise would have occurred. Governmental funds do *not* report capital assets (land, buildings and improvements, equipment, infrastructure, and intangibles), because such assets will be used in operations rather than converted to cash and therefore are not spendable.

Liabilities also are recognized in governmental funds only to the extent that they are expected to affect a government's near-term financing needs. A typical government, for instance, does not provide resources for debt service payments until the period in which payment is due. Usually, then, no liability is recognized in a governmental fund for the unmatured principal and accrued interest related to long-term debt. Likewise, a government's liabilities for vacation leave, claims and judgments, special termination benefits, and landfill closure and postclosure care costs are reported in the governmental funds in the period when payment becomes due.

The difference between assets and liabilities reported in a governmental fund is known as *fund balance*. Ideally, this amount represents the balance of financial resources available for appropriation at the end of the current fiscal period if the government budgeted on a basis consistent with GAAP. Two modifications are needed, however, before fund balance can serve this purpose.

First, not all *financial* resources reported in a governmental fund are *currently available* for appropriation. For example, long-term receivables associated with loans to other funds (advances receivable) are not converted to cash quickly enough to permit their appropriation in the near future. Likewise, while inventories and prepaid items may indirectly qualify as financial assets, they certainly are *not* available for spending. Therefore, a portion of fund balance must be reserved to indicate that such resources are *not* available for appropriation, even though they are reported in a governmental fund and so are reflected in fund balance.

Second, restrictions involving third parties can render financial resources unavailable for new spending. For example, a government may issue purchase orders or enter into contracts near the end of one fiscal period that it intends to honor in the subsequent fiscal period (i.e., encumbrances). These arrangements with third parties effectively prevent the amounts in question from being available for new spending. Thus, a portion of fund balance must be reserved to indicate the unavailability of such assets for appropriation.

Once all necessary reserves have been established, the remaining unreserved fund balance can serve as a measure of the financial resources available for appropriation had the government budgeted on a GAAP basis.

Governments have the *option* of designating all or a portion of unreserved fund balance to indicate that they already have tentative plans for using those resources. The critical distinction between reserved fund balance and *designated* unreserved fund balance is that the former involves some degree of *external* limitation on the use of resources (e.g., timing of cash flows, agreements with third parties), while the latter is subject solely to the government's discretion.

Exhibit 9 illustrates the structure of the governmental fund balance sheet.

EXHIBIT 9
Structure of the Governmental Fund
Balance Sheet

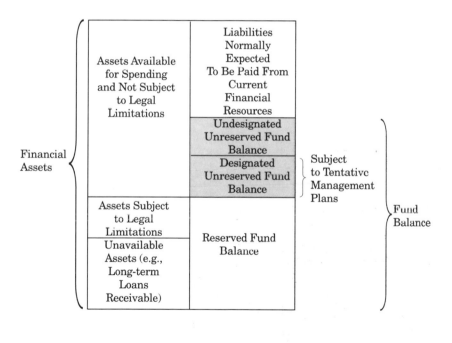

The governmental fund statement of revenues, expenditures, and changes in fund balances is used to report all transactions, events, and interfund activity that increase or decrease fund balances.

Certain increases and decreases in fund balances are classified separately from revenues and expenditures as *other financing sources* and *other financing uses* to avoid distorting regular ongoing revenue and expenditure trends. *Other financing sources* include proceeds of long-term debt, amounts transferred from other funds, and proceeds of the sale of capital assets (if not classified as a special item).

Also, GAAP require that a capital lease be reported as though resources had been borrowed from a third party and then remitted to the vendor. Accordingly, governmental funds report an *other financing source* and an expenditure equal to the amount of the net present value of the minimum lease payments at the inception of a capital lease agreement.

Other financing uses include the transfer of resources to another fund; the redemption of outstanding debt using resources provided by refunding debt (i.e., a current refunding); and the placement of the proceeds of refunding bonds into an escrow account for the redemption of outstanding debt at a specified future date (i.e., an advance refunding).

Budgetary comparison. GAAP require that a budgetary comparison be provided in connection with the basic financial statement for the general fund and any major individual special revenue funds. GAAP prescribe that this budgetary comparison be reported as RSI. Alternatively, GAAP specifically *permit* this budgetary comparison to be included as a third basic financial statement for the governmental funds. In this latter case, the budgetary comparison would fall within the scope of the independent audit of the financial statements. Conversely, RSI is specifically excluded from the scope of the audit, although auditors are responsible for performing certain limited procedures in regard to RSI (e.g., making inquiries of management regarding RSI measurement and presentation).

What is the purpose of the governmental fund financial statements?

Most decisions involving governmental (tax-supported) activities are made in the context of the annual or biennial appropriated operating budget, where the focus is on meeting a government's near-term financing needs. Governmental funds, with their distinctive emphasis on inflows and outflows of spendable resources, provide information uniquely useful for making decisions in a budgetary context. For example, governmental funds report a number of transactions that are significant from a budgetary or financing perspective, but that do *not* appear in the government-wide statement of activities. Such items include receipt of the proceeds of long-term debt, construction and other capital outlays, and debt service principal payments.

Conversely, governmental funds do *not* report a number of items that appear in the government-wide statement of activities because they typically are considered irrelevant for budgetary purposes. Such items include depreciation, amortization of debt-related premiums and discounts, and amortization of debt issuance costs.

What is the meaning of a deficit unreserved fund balance?

A deficit unreserved fund balance occurs whenever the available financial resources in a governmental fund are insufficient to cover the liabilities normally expected to be paid from those resources. A deficit unreserved fund balance should always be taken seriously as a possible indication that the government may have difficulty meeting its obligations in a timely manner. There are, however, at least two situations in which a deficit unreserved fund balance may *not* indicate potential financing problems.

Governments sometimes encumber the entire amount of a construction contract scheduled to proceed over the course of several fiscal periods. In that case, a deficit unreserved fund balance may result if a government does not finance the entire multi-year project up front. In that situation, the resulting deficit reflects no more than the government's intent to fund a portion of the long-term construction contract in future years (e.g., by issuing bonds), and it need not be considered a sign of potential financing problems.

Also, as noted, governmental funds ordinarily do *not* report long-term liabilities. GAAP specifically require, however, that borrowings from other funds always be reported as a liability of the borrowing governmental fund, even when the interfund borrowing is long-term in character. As a result, a deficit unreserved fund balance may occur simply because a governmental fund borrowed needed resources internally rather than from an external source. Once again, a deficit unreserved fund balance in such a case would *not* necessarily signal potential financing problems for the fund.

What is the meaning of an excess of expenditures over revenues in a governmental fund?

Governmental funds are expected to raise sufficient revenues in each period to cover the expenditures of that period. An excess of expenditures over revenues may indicate that a fund is living beyond its means. There are, however, a number of valid reasons why expenditures may properly exceed revenues in a given fiscal period. Examples of such reasons include:

- *"Budgeting" fund balance.* Budgeting involves the use of estimates. Naturally, the conservative use of revenue estimates over time can produce a significant fund balance surplus. While it is usually good financial practice to maintain a healthy fund balance surplus, such amounts may eventually exceed a government's needs as expressed in its fund balance policy. In that case, a government may decide to fund a portion of the annual or biennial appropriated operating budget with existing fund balance (budgeting fund balance) rather than by raising new resources, thereby putting fund balance back within the range established by the government's fund balance policy. In such cases, an excess of expenditures over revenues will occur in the year in which fund balance is *budgeted* in place of additional revenues. Clearly, it would be wrong to interpret such a planned reduction of fund balance as an indication of a potential financing problem.

- *Up-front contributions for capital projects.* Sometimes grantors or other contributors provide resources up front for capital projects that will continue over several fiscal periods. In that case, there typically will be a large excess of revenues over expenditures in the project's first fiscal period, followed in subsequent periods by an excess of expenditures over revenues. Such operating deficits resulting from the upfront funding of capital projects should not, of course, be considered an indication of potential financing problems. The same phenomenon occurs when governments deliberately build up fund balance over a number of periods to finance a major project.

- *Debt-financed capital projects.* It is common for governments to issue debt to finance capital construction and other capital acquisition. Because the proceeds of debt are reported as an *other financing source* rather than as *revenue*, a governmental fund used to report such a project typically would report an excess of expenditures over revenues. This excess of expenditures over revenues indicates only that the project is being financed through debt rather than through a government's regular revenues and does *not* indicate potential financing problems.

- *Expenditure-driven (reimbursement) grants.* Sometimes governments become eligible for grant resources by incurring qualifying expenditures. Such arrangements are commonly referred to as *expenditure-driven grants* or *reimbursement grants*. While a government is eligible for reimbursement in such situations as soon as qualifying expenditures have been incurred, it *cannot* recognize the related revenue until it actually becomes available for spending. Accordingly, an excess of expenditures over revenues may result simply from a grantor's delay in reimbursing a government's grant-related expenditures, which normally does *not* indicate potential financing problems.

- *Operating subsidies.* It is common for one fund to provide a subsidy to another fund. Such interfund subsidies are reported in state and local government financial statements as transfers (i.e., *an other financing source*) rather than as revenue. Expenditures exceeding revenues for a given governmental fund need not indicate a financing problem if it is the government's policy to provide regular operating subsidies to finance the difference. However, transfers that do *not* reflect a government's policy to provide ongoing operating subsidies to a given fund should be carefully examined to ensure that they do not represent a stopgap measure that may be masking a serious financing problem.

Why are the numbers that appear in the governmental fund financial statements different from those that appear for governmental activities in the government-wide financial statements?

For various reasons, the numbers reported in the governmental fund financial statements differ from those reported for governmental activities in the government-wide financial statements. The most important of these reasons are summarized here:

Financial assets versus total assets. The governmental fund balance sheet reports only *financial assets*, while the government-wide statement of net assets reports *all* of a government's assets, *including capital assets*.

Liabilities that are due and payable. The governmental fund balance sheet reports only liabilities that are due and payable with current available financial resources. Accordingly, governmental funds typically do *not* report liabilities for unmatured long-term debt, vacation leave, claims and judgments, special termination benefits, and landfill closure and postclosure care costs. Conversely, the government-wide statement of net assets reports *all* of a government's liabilities, regardless of when they mature.

Capital outlay versus depreciation. The governmental statement of revenues, expenditures, and changes in fund balances reports an expenditure when capital assets are constructed or purchased. The government-wide statement of activities, on the other hand, reports depreciation expense over the useful life of capital assets.

Debt issuance and principal repayment. The governmental fund statement of revenues, expenditures, and changes in fund balances reports an inflow of resources (i.e., receipt of debt proceeds) and an outflow of resources (i.e., debt service principal payments) in connection with debt issuance and subsequent repayment of principal. The government-wide statement of activities reports neither.

Immediate recognition versus deferral and amortization. The governmental fund statement of revenues, expenditures, and changes in fund balances reports issuance costs, premiums, and discounts when they first occur; the government-wide statement of activities spreads out recognition of these amounts over the related period. For example, governmental funds recognize debt issuance costs when they are paid, while the government-wide statement of activities recognizes an expense over the life of the related debt.

Revenue when available versus revenue when earned. Governmental funds recognize revenues only to the extent that related cash inflows are available to liquidate liabilities of the current period. The government-wide statement of activities recognizes revenues as soon as they are earned, regardless of when the cash is received.

Internal service fund activities. Internal service funds use the same accounting and financial reporting used by enterprise funds, so both are classified as *proprietary funds*. In most cases, however, governmental activities are the primary customers of a government's internal service funds. Thus, internal service funds normally are included as part of *governmental activities* in the government-wide financial statements, even though they are treated as proprietary funds in the fund-based financial statements.

GAAP require that governments present a simple reconciliation between the governmental fund financial statements and the government-wide financial statements. This reconciliation must be presented either on the face of the governmental fund financial statements or as an accompanying schedule. Governments present a more detailed reconciliation of these differences in the notes to the financial statements when the accounts being adjusted are not clearly evident.

A summary of the key differences between the governmental fund financial statements and the government-wide financial statements is presented in Exhibit 10.

EXHIBIT 10
Key Differences Between the
Governmental Fund Financial Statements
and the Government-Wide Financial Statements

Item	Treatment in Governmental Fund Statements	Treatment in Government-Wide Financial Statements
Financial Assets	Reported	Reported
Capital Assets	Not Reported	Reported
Liabilities That Are Due and Payable	Reported	Reported
Liabilities That Are *Not* Due and Payable	Not Reported	Reported
Capital Outlay	Reported	Not Reported
Depreciation	Not Reported	Reported
Receipt of Debt Proceeds	Reported	Not Reported
Debt Service Principal Payments	Reported	Not Reported
Issuance Costs, Premiums, and Discounts	Recognized as Incurred	Deferred and Amortized
Revenue Recognition	When Measurable and Available	When Earned (Even if Not Available)
Internal Service Funds	Not Reported as Governmental Funds	Normally Included as Part of Governmental Activities

Proprietary Fund Statements

What are the basic financial statements for proprietary funds?

There are three basic financial statements for proprietary funds: the statement of net assets; the statement of revenues, expenses, and changes in net assets; and the statement of cash flows.

Statement of net assets. The statement of net assets for proprietary funds is prepared in essentially the same way as the government-wide statement of net assets. Both report *all* assets and liabilities, including capital assets and long-term liabilities. One difference between the two statements, however, is that the proprietary fund statement of net assets always presents assets and liabilities on a classified basis. That is, current assets and liabilities are reported separate from long-term assets and liabilities. The government-wide statement of net assets, on the other hand, frequently presents assets and liabilities in the order of their relative liquidity (based on the average maturity of items within each class), although a classified presentation also is acceptable.

Current assets and liabilities normally are expected to mature within one year of the end of the fiscal period. An important exception to this general rule involves restricted assets (e.g., special accounts established to comply with revenue bond covenants), which are *not* included as part of *current assets* because of significant restrictions placed on their use. Likewise, liabilities to be repaid from restricted assets are not reported as *current liabilities* because their liquidation will involve the use of noncurrent (restricted assets) rather than current resources.

The difference between assets and liabilities is reported as net assets. Unlike private-sector businesses, which distinguish invested net assets (e.g., owner's equity, capital stock, paid-in-capital in excess of par) from accumulated profits (retained earnings), proprietary funds classify the various components of their net assets based on their accessibility for use. Thus a proprietary fund's net investment in its capital assets (capital assets less related debt) and its restricted resources (e.g., unspent grant proceeds) are reported separate from its unrestricted net assets (the same classifications used for net assets in the government-wide financial statements).

Proprietary funds may present a balance sheet rather than a statement of net assets. Even then, the difference between assets and liabilities should be reported as *net fund assets* or *net fund equity*.

Statement of revenues, expenses, and changes in net assets. All proprietary funds are intended to recover from customers a significant portion of the cost of providing goods and services. To help financial statement users assess the degree to which this goal has been achieved, the statement of revenues, expenses, and changes in net assets isolates *operating revenues* and *operating expenses* from other changes in net assets. Operating expenses represent the costs incurred to provide goods and services to customers (cost of goods sold or cost of services provided). Operating revenues represent the amounts received from customers in exchange for those goods and services. Accordingly, *operating income (loss)* serves as a measure of how sufficiently a given activity has been able to pay its own way.

A proprietary fund also commonly reports increases and decreases in its net assets that do not directly arise in connection with providing goods or services to customers. For example, a proprietary fund may receive a capital grant from another government (capital contribution), or an operating subsidy from the general fund (transfer). Likewise, proprietary funds may have extraordinary items or special items whose inclusion as part of operating revenues and operating expenses could distort trend data. All such nonoperating items are reported immediately following *operating income.*

Statement of cash flows. It is not enough that a proprietary fund recover all or a portion of its costs. It also must generate sufficient cash flows to meet its obligations in a timely manner. The cash flows statement allows financial statement users to assess the adequacy of a proprietary fund's cash flows.

Cash flows for proprietary funds are classified into four categories:

- *Cash flows from operating activities.* This category is used mostly to report cash inflows and outflows associated with operating revenues and operating expenses. Such cash flows would include cash received from customers, collections of receivables, cash paid to employees, cash paid to vendors, and liquidation of payables.

- *Cash flows from noncapital financing activities.* This category is used for items such as receipt of cash from grantors and other funds, receipt of debt proceeds from debt not associated with capital acquisition, and debt service payments on debt not associated with capital acquisition.

- *Cash flows from capital and capital-related financing activities.* This category is used for capital outlays, the receipt of debt proceeds from capital-related debt, debt-service payments on capital-related debt, and receipt of proceeds from the sale of capital assets.

- *Cash flows from investing activities.* This category is used for the purchase and sale of investments, interest earnings, and receipt of dividends.

The statement of cash flows includes or is accompanied by a reconciliation that summarizes the reasons why *cash from operating activities* is different from *operating income.* Some of the most common reasons for these differences are illustrated in Exhibit 11.

EXHIBIT 11
Common Differences Between Operating Income
and Cash Flows from Operating Activities

Transaction	Effect on Operating Income	Effect on Cash Flows from Operating Activities	Adjustment That Needs To Be Made to Operating Income in Reconciliation	Elements of Reconciliation Start: Operating Income
Sales on Credit (i.e., Creation of Accounts Receivable)	Increase	None	Subtract to Arrive at Net Cash Flows	Subtract Net Increase in Receivables (or Add Net Decrease in Receivables)
Collection of Receivables	None	Increase	Add to Arrive at Net Cash Flows	
Incurrence of Payables and Other Operating Liabilities	Decrease	None	Add to Arrive at Net Cash Flows	Subtract Net Decrease in Liabilities (or Add Net Increase in Liabilities)
Liquidation of Payables and Other Operating Liabilities	None	Decrease	Subtract to Arrive at Net Cash Flows	
Purchase of Inventories	None	Decrease	Subtract to Arrive at Net Cash Flows	Subtract Net Increase in Inventories (or Add Net Decrease in Inventories)
Consumption of Inventories	Decrease	None	Add to Arrive at Net Cash Flows	
Depreciation Expense	Decrease	None	Add to Arrive at Net Cash Flows	Add Back Depreciation Expense and Amortization Expense
Amortization Expense	Decrease	None	Add to Arrive at Net Cash Flows	
				Finish: Net Cash Flows from Operating Activities

Should all enterprise funds be self-supporting?

Enterprise funds are used only when a government intends for user fees and charges to fund at least a substantial portion of the cost of providing goods and services. Still, there are significant and legitimate differences in the financing goals that governments set for different enterprise funds.

Some activities, of course, are intended to be fully self-financing. For example, many public utilities are required by law or management policy to recover the full cost of providing services through user fees and charges. In other cases, however, a government may intend for user charges to finance only a portion of the cost of providing goods and services. Such situations are especially common when a given service (e.g., public transportation) provides direct benefits to users as well as *substantial indirect benefits* to the public at large (e.g., decreased traffic congestion, decreased need for road construction and maintenance, decreased need for parking, decreased air pollution levels, increased availability of transportation for low-income citizens).

It clearly is a cause for concern when an enterprise fund intended to be fully financed by fees and charges proves unable to pay its own way. Such is not the case, however, for enterprise funds intended to be partially self-financing. In this case, concern is warranted only when the size of the subsidy exceeds the indirect benefits to the public. Of course, elected officials must ultimately determine the appropriate subsidy level.

What is the meaning of a significant ongoing surplus or deficit in an internal service fund?

Internal service funds, in contrast to enterprise funds, are designed to serve as cost-allocation devices. That is, the role of an internal service fund is to accumulate the costs associated with providing a particular service (e.g., motor pool) and then to charge those who use that service for their fair share of the cost. Ideally, an internal service fund should break even (revenues should equal expenses). In practice, however, it is appropriate for an internal service fund to maintain a small surplus to ensure adequate working capital as well as sufficient resources to replace capital assets used to provide services (e.g., charges to users based on estimated replacement cost rather than historical cost depreciation).

While a temporary surplus or deficit in an internal service fund should not cause concern, substantial, long-term surpluses or deficits ought to raise questions regarding the calculation of user charges. For example, an ongoing material surplus in an internal service fund could represent an attempt to use the internal service fund as a secret reserve. At very least it raises issues regarding the fairness of the amount reported as expenses or expenditures in the user funds.

Indeed, such a surplus could cause grantors to disallow a portion of any related costs charged to their programs. Even more troubling, an ongoing material deficit in an internal service fund may indicate that equity (e.g., fund balance) may be overstated in the user funds, given that user charges clearly have *not* been sufficient to cover related expenses. In that case, the internal service fund may need to be terminated.

Fiduciary Fund Statements

What are the basic financial statements for fiduciary funds?

There are two basic financial statements for fiduciary funds: the statement of fiduciary net assets and the statement of changes in fiduciary net assets. Agency funds are reported only in the statement of fiduciary net assets.

The statement of fiduciary net assets reports all assets and liabilities associated with the fiduciary funds. The difference between assets and liabilities is reported as *net assets*. Unlike proprietary funds, fiduciary funds are *not* required to divide their net assets into separate components based on their availability for use in operations.

The statement of changes in fiduciary net assets reports *all* changes in the net assets of fiduciary funds without distinguishing earnings-related changes (i.e., revenues and expenses) from other types of changes. Consequently, all changes in fiduciary net assets are classified as *additions* and *deductions*. Further, costs associated with investment activities are reported as an adjustment (decrease) to investment income in the *additions* section of the statement of changes in fiduciary net assets rather than as separate items in the *deductions* section of that statement.

As noted, agency funds are *not* included in the statement of changes in fiduciary net assets because by definition all assets in an agency fund are offset by a corresponding liability. Therefore, since assets and liabilities are always equal, there is no balance of net assets for which changes can be reported.

Also as noted, fiduciary activities are *excluded* from the government-wide financial statements because the resources reported in fiduciary funds are not available to support the government's programs.

Does a positive balance in net assets for a defined benefit pension trust fund indicate that the plan is fully funded?

A defined benefit pension plan promises specific benefits to employees after retirement based on a predetermined benefit formula. These benefits are financed by a combination of contributions (from employers and sometimes from employees) and investment earnings.

The present value of the pension benefits earned by employees based on service already performed is known as the *actuarial accrued liability*. This amount is an *actuarial* liability rather than an *accounting* liability and therefore is *not* reported on the statement of fiduciary net assets. Consequently, the statement of fiduciary net assets presents the assets that have been accumulated to pay pension benefits but *not* the present value of the pension benefits to be paid from those assets. Therefore, a positive balance in net assets for a defined benefit pension plan trust fund does *not* indicate that the plan is fully funded (i.e., assets equal or exceed the actuarial accrued liability).

Financial statement users desiring to know the degree to which a defined benefit pension plan has been funded should consult the schedule of funding progress, which is presented as RSI. That schedule compares the *actuarial* value of plan assets (i.e., an average of the market value of plan assets over a specified period) and the actuarial accrued liability over time, expressing the former as a percentage of the latter (e.g., 90 percent funded).

Required Supplementary Information

What are the essential components of a budgetary comparison?

A budgetary comparison must be presented in connection with the basic financial statements for the general fund and any major individual special revenue funds. The key components of that presentation are:

- Expenditures and revenues as approved in the original appropriated budget (i.e., generally the budget passed prior to the start of the fiscal period);

- Expenditures and revenues per the final amended version of the appropriated budget at the end of the fiscal period; and

- Actual expenditures and revenues calculated using the same basis of accounting used for budgeting (e.g., cash basis, cash basis plus encumbrances, modified accrual basis, modified accrual basis plus encumbrances).

Governments commonly present a separate column to report variances between the final amended budget and actual amounts, although they are not required to do so.

What is the meaning of a significant difference between the original budget and the final amended budget?

The annual or biennial appropriated budget normally is approved *prior* to the start of the fiscal period, so a government must rely on its best *estimates* of resource inflows and outflows for the coming fiscal period. The original budget, then, often must be amended to reflect subsequent developments.

In some cases, significant differences between the original budget and the final amended budget may indicate a weakness in the budget process. For example, budgetary amendments may be needed because a government has failed to fully integrate the process used for developing the operating budget with its other planning activities (e.g., capital budgeting, strategic planning).

Usually, however, budgetary amendments represent an appropriate response to unforeseeable changes in a government's circumstances. For example, a government highly dependent on a volatile revenue source such as sales tax might need to amend its operating budget in response to changes in the economy. In the same way, a major plant closing may require a budgetary amendment to reflect a decrease in tax revenues *and* an increase in expenditures related to government services to the unemployed.

Accordingly, great care must be exercised in interpreting the significance of changes between the original budget and the final amended budget. Any analysis of such changes should always begin with careful consideration of management's discussion of budgetary changes presented in management's discussion and analysis.

How should variances be interpreted in the budgetary comparison?

One goal of the budgetary comparison is to permit financial statement users to compare actual revenues and expenditures with the final amended budget. Indeed, most governments voluntarily present a separate column as part of the budgetary comparison presentation to highlight variances. Care must be taken, however, to avoid misinterpreting the true significance of variances.

The goal of most private-sector business enterprises is to maximize profit (i.e., excess of revenues over expenses). Therefore, anything that increases revenues or decreases expenses may properly be considered favorable to the business. The profit motive, however, is absent from the public sector, where the goal is to provide services. For state and local governments, revenues are a means to an end rather than an end in themselves; so, there is nothing inherently favorable about reducing expenditures as a result of reducing services. Likewise, there is nothing inherently favorable about generating revenues in excess of a government's needs.

Users of state and local government financial statements, then, should avoid applying private-sector notions of variance analysis to the budgetary comparison of a state or local government. To help minimize the possibility of misinterpreting the significance of variances, governments often attempt to use neutral or arithmetic terminology such as *positive* and *negative* or *over* and *under* to describe the variance column, rather than more subjective terms like *favorable* and *unfavorable* commonly encountered in private-sector cost accounting.

What are the purpose and meaning of the required supplementary information presented for defined benefit pension plans?

As noted, a defined benefit pension plan promises specific benefits to employees after retirement based on a predetermined benefit formula. Participating employees and others with an interest in the pension plan will wish to make their own assessment of the pension plan's ability to pay benefits to employees. Therefore, the presentation of two schedules of actuarial trend data to permit financial statement users to make such an assessment is required.

Schedule of funding progress. The key to assessing a pension plan's eventual ability to make timely payments to beneficiaries, as promised, is to compare the accumulated assets of the pension plan with the present value of estimated future benefit payments. The values needed to make a valid comparison for this purpose, however, are the *actuarially calculated amounts* rather than the *accounting amounts* reported on the statement of plan net assets.

Thus, the *actuarial value* of plan assets is based on their *average fair value over time*, whereas accountants report plan assets on the statement of net assets based on their *fair value at a point in time* (i.e., the end of the fiscal period). Likewise, the *actuarial accrued liability* represents the full measure of benefits owed to employees based upon services rendered, whereas an *accounting liability* is reported only to the extent that benefits are due and payable (pension plans) or that annual required contributions are not fully funded (employees).

The schedule of funding progress is designed to allow financial statement users to directly compare the *actuarial* value of plan assets with the *actuarial* accrued liability. The difference between these numbers is then highlighted in two ways. First, the difference between the two amounts is reported separately on the schedule of funding progress. Since pension plans are systematically funded over many years, it is common for the actuarial accrued liability to exceed the actuarial value of plan assets, resulting in an *unfunded* actuarial accrued liability even in situations where employers consistently fund 100 percent of their annual required contribution to the pension plan.

Second, the degree to which the actuarial accrued liability has been funded is highlighted by reporting the actuarial value of plan assets as a percentage of the actuarial accrued liability (*funded ratio*). These concepts are illustrated in Exhibit 12.

EXHIBIT 12
Nature of the Unfunded Actuarial Accrued Liability

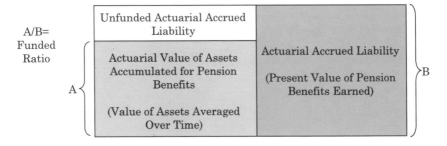

Financial statement users need some point of reference to be able to assess the significance of the unfunded actuarial accrued liability for a particular pension plan. Accordingly, the schedule of funding progress compares the unfunded actuarial accrued liability to that portion of the employer's payroll covered by the pension plan. Thus, an employer may report that the unfunded actuarial accrued liability represents 50 percent or 150 percent of covered payroll, just as a homeowner might indicate that house payments represent 35 percent of gross pay.

The key factors in evaluating funding progress for pension plans are the direction in which the funding ratio is headed and the rate at which progress is occurring. Both factors can only be assessed *over time.* So information on a pension plan's funding progress must be presented as trend data over a period of years.

Assume, for example, that one pension plan is now 90 percent funded, while another pension plan is only 85 percent funded. At first, a financial statement user might be tempted to assume that the first pension plan is making better funding progress than the second. This would *not* be the case, however, if the first pension plan was 100 percent funded just five years ago, when the second plan was only 70 percent funded. The trend data provided on the schedule of funding progress is essential for assessing the true significance of a pension plan's funding progress.

No schedule of funding progress is presented in connection with defined benefit pension plans that use the *aggregate actuarial cost allocation methodology*, since that methodology does *not* involve the separate calculation of an unfunded actuarial accrued liability.

Schedule of employer contributions. Employers finance their pension promises by making annual, actuarially determined pension contributions. By definition, a defined benefit pension plan should have adequate accumulated resources to pay all of its pension benefits in a timely manner as long as each year's annual required contribution (ARC) is fully funded, provided that the actuarial assumptions used to calculate the ARC prove sound. Consequently, a pattern of fully funding the ARC is another key indicator that a pension plan's resources will be adequate to make promised benefit payments.

The schedule of employer contributions provides the information that financial statement users need to determine whether an employer is consistently funding the ARC. Accordingly, the ARC and actual contributions are compared over several years, with the actual amount funded being expressed as a percentage of the ARC. A pattern of full (100 percent) funding is a good indicator that a pension plan's assets will be adequate to make pension benefit payments in full and in a timely manner.

What are the purpose and meaning of the required supplementary information presented for infrastructure assets?

Infrastructure assets, usually treated the same way as other capital assets, initially are capitalized at their historical cost and subsequently depreciated over the estimated useful lives of the assets. Still, governments have the *option* of avoiding the requirement to report depreciation expense for networks or subsystems of infrastructure assets that meet the following requirements:

- The government must have an up-to-date inventory of the assets of those networks and subsystems.

- The government must perform or obtain condition assessments of those assets and summarize the results using a measurement scale. It is essential that such condition assessments be replicable (i.e., conducted using methods that would allow different measurers to reach substantially similar results).

- The government must make an annual estimate of the amount needed to maintain and preserve those assets at a condition level established and disclosed by the government.

- The government must document that infrastructure assets are being preserved at or above the condition level established and disclosed by the government.

Governments electing this option—or *modified approach* to infrastructure reporting—for one or more networks or subsystems of infrastructure assets are required to present two types of information regarding those assets. First, they must present the *results of the three most recently completed condition assessments* to demonstrate that infrastructure assets have been maintained at or above the condition level established by the government. Second, they must disclose both their estimates of the amount needed to maintain or preserve infrastructure assets at the level established by the government and actual amounts of expense *for each of the past five reporting periods*. The purpose of this second schedule is to allow users of the financial statements to make their own assessment of the government's long-term commitment to maintaining those infrastructure assets.

APPENDIX A

Comparison of the Traditional and New
Governmental Financial Reporting Models

Item	Traditional Model	New Model
Terminology for minimum GAAP presentation	General purpose financial statements	Basic financial statements
Highest level of aggregation/consolidation	Combined financial statements (data presented by fund type)	Government-wide financial statements
Measurement focus for governmental funds/activities	Current financial resources	Funds=current financial resources Government-wide=economic resources
Basis of accounting for governmental funds/activities	Modified accrual	Funds=modified accrual Government-wide=accrual
General capital assets (other than infrastructure)	Reported in general fixed assets account group and not depreciated	Reported in government-wide financial statements and depreciated
General infrastructure assets	Reporting optional	Reported in government-wide financial statements and (normally) depreciated
General long-term liabilities	Reported in general long-term debt account group	Reported in government-wide financial statements
Focus of fund reporting	Fund types	Major funds (governmental and enterprise funds) Fund types (internal service and fiduciary funds)
Governmental fund types	General, special revenue, capital projects and debt service	General, special revenue, capital projects, debt service and permanent
Equity of proprietary funds	Contributed capital and retained earnings	Net assets
Reporting cash flows from operating activities in the statement of cash flows	Direct method or indirect method	Direct method

(continued on page 72)

Appendix A, continued

Item	Traditional Model	New Model
Segment information	Required in a variety of situations for individual enterprise funds	Required for individual enterprise funds or identifiable activities within an individual enterprise fund for which revenue-backed debt with an identifiable revenue stream is outstanding
Fiduciary fund types	Expendable trust, nonexpendable trust, pension trust, investment trust and agency	Private-purpose trust, pension trust, investment trust and agency
Escheat assets	Reported in expendable trust fund	Reported in private-purpose trust fund
State unemployment compensation benefit plans	Reported in expendable trust fund	Reported in enterprise fund
IRC Section 457 deferred compensation plans	Reported in expendable trust fund	Reported in pension (and other employee benefits) trust fund
Transfers	Residual equity and operating (2 categories)	Transfers (1 category)
Object of budgetary comparison	Final amended budget	Both original and final amended budget
Focus of budgetary comparison	Governmental fund type	General fund and major individual special revenue funds
Status of budgetary comparison	Basic financial statement	Required supplementary information (Option to report as basic financial statement)
Narrative introduction, overview and analysis	Not required	Management's discussion and analysis (required supplementary information)
Colleges and universities	Option to use specialized reporting model	Use governmental reporting model
Governmental entities using not-for-profit accounting	Option to use specialized reporting model	Use governmental reporting model

APPENDIX B

Index

Actuarial accrued liability (defined benefit pension plans)
Defined 69-70

Agency funds
Not included in statement of changes in fiduciary net assets 59-60

Avoidable costs
Compared to unavoidable costs 36-39

Budgetary comparison
Essential components 62
Meaning of difference between original and final amended budget 63
Meaning of variances 63
Optional presentation as basic governmental fund financial statement 41-44

Budgeting fund balance
As cause of excess of expenditures over revenues 47-49

Business enterprise model 8-9

Business-type activities
Reported separately from governmental activities in the government-wide financial statements 32

Capital costs 36-39

Cash flows from operating activities
Reconciliation to operating income 56

Cash flows reporting
Description of statement of cash flows for proprietary funds 53-56

Cost data
Interpretation 36-39

Debt-financed capital projects
As cause of excess of expenditures over revenues 47-49

Deficit in internal service fund
    Meaning 58

Deficit "unreserved fund balance"
    Meaning 46

Deficit "unrestricted net assets"
    Meaning 33-34

Depreciation expense
    Compared to replacement cost 36-39
    Role in rate setting 36-39

Direct costs
    Compared to indirect costs 36-39

Enterprise funds
    Degree of self-financing required 57

Excess of expenditures over revenues (governmental funds)
    Meaning 47-49

Expenditure-driven grants
    As cause of excess of expenditures over revenues 47-49

Extraordinary items
    Defined 40

Fiduciary funds
    Basic financial statements 59-60
    Not included within government-wide financial state-
        ments 31

Final amended budget
    Meaning of differences from original budget 63

Financial Accounting Standards Board (FASB)
    Sets GAAP for business enterprises and not-for-profit or-
        ganizations 6-7

Financial reporting models (see governmental financial re-
    porting model)
    Definition and elements 6-7
    Need for separate governmental model 10
    Number of models 8-9
    Scope 7

Fixed costs 36-39

Generally accepted accounting principles (GAAP)
    Criteria for financial reporting 6-7

Governmental activities
    Reconciliation to governmental funds 50-52
    Reported separately from business-type activities in government-wide financial statements 32

Government Finance Officers Association (GFOA)
    Position on infrastructure reporting 3-4

Governmental fund balance sheet
    Described 41-44
    Structure 43

Governmental fund financial statements
    Described 41-44
    Differences from "governmental activities" in government-wide financial statements 52
    Purpose 45

Governmental fund statement of revenues, expenditures, and changes in fund balances
    Described 41-44

Government-wide financial statements
    Description 26-29
    Need to separate governmental and business-type activities 32
    Purpose 30
    Scope 31

Governmental Accounting Standards Board (GASB)
    Sets GAAP for governments 6-7

Governmental financial reporting model
    Basic structure 18-22
    Key features summarized Introduction, 12-17
    Need for separate model 10
    Need for new model 12-17
    Relationship to the comprehensive annual financial report 22

Indirect costs
    Compared to direct costs 36-39

Infrastructure assets
    GFOA position on infrastructure reporting Introduction
    Modified approach 65-68
    Related RSI 65-68

Internal service funds
    Meaning of significant surplus or deficit 58
Management's discussion and analysis (MD&A)
    Contents 24
    Purpose 23
    Reliability 25
Modified approach (infrastructure reporting)
    GFOA position (Introduction)
    Related RSI 65-68
Net assets
    Categories 26-29
Net cost format (government-wide statement of activities) 26-29
Not-for-profit model 8-9
Operating income
    Reconciliation to "cash flows from operating activities" 56
Operating subsidies
    As cause of excess of expenditures over revenues 47-49
Original
    Meaning of differences from final amended budget 63
    Other financing sources/uses
    Described 41-44
Pension plans
    Related RSI 69-70
Pension trust fund
    Meaning of surplus 61
Program revenues (government-wide statement of activities) 26-29
Proprietary funds
    Basic financial statements 53-56
Rate setting
    Role of depreciation expense 36-39
Reconciliation
    Governmental funds and governmental activities 50-52
Reimbursement grants
    As cause of excess of expenditures over revenues 47-49

Replacement cost
    Compared to depreciation expense 36-39
Schedule of employer contributions (defined benefit pension plans)
    Described 69-70
Schedule of funding progress (defined benefit pension plans)
    Described 69-70
Special items
    Defined 40
Statement of activities (government-wide financial statements)
    Description 26-29
    Net cost format 26-29
Statement of cash flows (proprietary funds)
    Description 53-56
    Reconciliation of operating income to cash flows from operating activities 56
Statement of changes in fiduciary net assets
    Description 59-60
Statement of fiduciary net assets
    Description 59-60
Statement of net assets (government-wide financial statements)
    Categories of net assets 26-29
    Description 26-29
    Elements 28
    Order of presentation of assets and liabilities 26-29
Statement of net assets (proprietary funds)
    Description 53-56
Statement of revenues, expenses, and changes in net assets (proprietary funds)
    Description 53-56
Sunken costs 36-39
Surplus
    Meaning in internal service fund 58
    Meaning in pension trust fund 61
Unavoidable costs
    Compared to avoidable costs 36-39

Unfunded actuarial accrued liability
    Defined 69-70
    Nature 66
Unreserved fund balance
    Meaning of deficit balance 46
Unrestricted net assets
    Meaning of deficit balance 33-34
    Meaning of positive balance 35
Upfront contributions for capital projects
    As cause of excess of expenditures over revenues 47-49
Variances
    Meaning in budgetary comparisons 64